THE

American Union Commission:

ITS

ORIGIN, OPERATIONS AND PURPOSES.

ORGANIZED TO AID IN THE RESTORATION OF THE UNION UPON THE BASIS OF FREEDOM, INDUSTRY, EDUCATION, AND CHRISTIAN MORALITY.

CENTRAL OFFICE:
No. 14 BIBLE HOUSE, NEW YORK CITY.
BRANCH OFFICES:
165 PEARL ST., BOSTON. 1210 CHESTNUT ST., PHILADELPHIA.
89 AND 91 WEST BALTIMORE STREET, BALTIMORE.
90 WASHINGTON STREET, CHICAGO.

OCTOBER, 1865.

New York:
SANFORD, HARROUN & CO., STEAM JOB PRINTERS, 644 BROADWAY, COR. BLEECKER.

1865.

Letter from Maj.-Gen. O. O. Howard, Chief of Bureau for Refugees, Freedmen, and Abandoned Lands.

"*Rev. Lyman Abbott, Secretary American Union Commission.*

"Dear Sir:—Many questions are propounded to me as to whether the Bureau, of which I am in charge, embraces in its work the poor whites of the South. I answer, it does so far as that applies to the loyal refugees. This is all that is warranted by the law under which I am acting. Yet when ever any cases of necessity and suffering are presented to me regarding these people, I always appeal to your association for aid. Everything that you, as a commission, can do to facilitate industrial pursuits, to encourage education, and meet the wants of the suffering amongst the poor white people, who have been degraded by slavery, is collateral with my speciality, and meets my hearty sympathy and support.

The work of elevating the poor people of the South, of all classes, is the privilege—nay more, it is the duty of all true men in this transition period of our history as a nation. It is well to bear in mind, particularly amongst our Christian people, and at a time when public sentiment is likely to be absorbed by other objects of interest, that duty requires them to remember those suffering poor, and make their contributions to meet their pressing wants. The Union Commission affords facilities adequate to this important work, and it becomes the Christian churches to examine carefully the fields that demand the sort of labor referred to, and to seek earnestly and prayerfully to discharge the responsibilities, now more than ever devolving upon them, respecting this matter. Every assistance given to industry and education affords direct and indirect aid in the solution of the difficult problems affecting the Freedmen. What we need at the South is Christian charity. All you can do to promote this spirit is positive help, and every block of prejudice removed clears the way for real, substantial progress. I trust your efforts will receive every encouragement and the Divine blessing.

"Very respectfully,
"O. O. HOWARD,
"Major General, Commissioner, &c.

"Aug. 28th, 1865."

Letter from Maj.-Gen. A. E. Burnside.

"Providence, R. I., Friday, Aug. 4th, 1865.

"*Rev. Lyman Abbott, General Secretary American Union Commission.*

"My Dear Sir:—I am in receipt of your circular, and beg to express to you my great happiness at hearing of your organization. It will be followed in its work by the prayers of all the loyal people in the country. Made up, as it is, of the late workers in those two great charities, the Sanitary and Christian Commissions, it cannot fail to do great good.

"Sincerely your friend,
"A. E. BURNSIDE."

THE AMERICAN UNION COMMISSION.

Its Origin, Objects, and Operations.

In June, 1864, Rev. Joseph P. Thompson, D.D., and Rev. Wm. I. Buddington, D.D., visited Tennessee as delegates of the Christian Commission. They witnessed the desolate condition of the country, the fences gone, implements of industry destroyed, houses burnt, churches and school houses standing idle or used for military purposes, while thousands of wretched refugees crowded Nashville and Louisville. The necessity of some organization to aid in rebuilding the places laid waste by war, as well as in giving temporary assistance to those who had suffered from it, was apparent. They consulted with Andrew Johnson, then Governor of Tennessee, upon the subject, who strongly urged its importance; returned to New York to lay the partially developed plan before some leading citizens there; perfected the nucleus of an organization; and visited personally President Lincoln, who not only gave the plan his warmest approval, but interlined in the proposed constitution, with his own hand, a phrase of his own suggestion. At the same time the War Department gave it the same facilities of transportation, &c., awarded to the Sanitary and Christian Commissions. Thus the Union Commission has not only received the approval of both the late and the present President, but both of them participated in its formation.

Organization.—This consists of branches established in the principal cities of the Union, from which delegates are elected who constitute the Commission, elect its officers and direct its affairs.

Refugees.—Thousands of these, driven from their homes by the surging of contending armies, or the persecution of guerillas, escaped to our lines and were brought by government to the North. Sick, hungry, half naked, they were left upon the wharves of Cairo, Louisville and Cincinnati to die, or huddled uncared for in camps at Nashville, Memphis, Vicksburgh and other points. Many of them were loyal. Over three thousand women and children were gathered by government at Clarksville, from the mountain regions of the South, whose husbands and brothers had enlisted in the Union Army, leaving them to the mercy of the merciless guerilla. For these unfortunates, barracks were obtained from government, and rations were furnished. The people of the North were appealed to for aid. They responded generously. In temporary homes at Cairo, Cincinnati, Louisville, Chicago, Baltimore and New York, these people were received. They were cleansed, fed, clothed, the sick were cared for and the well were provided with permanent homes and employment in the country. Thus, by the charities of the North the Commission has been enabled to provide permanently for from seventy-five to a hundred thousand refugees, and to relieve the country from the evils of a gigantic pauperism. This work is now over; these barracks are now all closed.

Special Relief.—While the Commission was thus providing for refugees, the work of war went on with a rapidity quite unparalleled in history. Sherman marched unopposed from Atlanta to Savannah, from Savannah to Goldsboro. Savannah, Charleston, Wilmington. and finally Richmond fell into the hands of the Government. An immense train of refugees, black and white followed the Federal Army. The Union Commission entered the Southern field thus opened to it, and commenced its more comprehensive work. It sent a special agent to Savannah, another to Charleston, and another to Richmond. It sent supplies to other points to be distributed by the agents of the Sanitary and Christian Commissions, whose most efficient co-operation has always been given for the purpose. Thus it has sent supplies of food and clothing throughout the South, as far West as Little Rock, as far South as Fernandina, &c. The people have generously given us the means for these benefactions. In a little over a year the Commission has raised nearly $150,000 in money and supplies, nearly all of which, however, are now distributed. We have thus aided, as nearly as we can estimate, twenty thousand suffering poor in middle Tennessee; an incalculable number in East Tennessee and Western Virginia, chiefly through the New England Branch; over fifteen thousand in and about Richmond; and through the Baltimore Branch have distributed nearly two thousand school books and Bibles, over thirteen hundred garments, besides seed and implements, in all over five thousand dollars worth, chiefly in the Valley of the Shenandoah. Smaller stores have been sent to other points.

The necessity for this work is far from over. Official reports, extracts from which are appended, show already that in certain regions the greatest destitution already exists, and give ground for the greatest apprehensions of actual starvation and death in many instances this winter, unless relief is afforded from the North.

Industry and Emigration.—While we have thus been sending supplies of food and clothing to the destitute, we have also sent seed and implements for distribution by careful and sagacious agents, to those who are desirous of going to work, but are without the means of labor. At the same time we have opened in New York City a bureau of information for the benefit of such as wish to emigrate South. Here are to be found copies of the leading Southern newspapers, government maps of the Southern States, and detailed information as to business openings, prices and character of lands, &c., gleaned from official reports and extensive correspondence.

Education.—By our contributions of special supplies we have opened the way for the more permanent and important work of education. The war has effectually destroyed such systems of public instruction as formerly existed. The school funds, either appropriated to military purposes, or converted into confederate bonds, are nearly all lost. The school houses, standing idle, or used as military hospitals and prisons are in sad want of repair. The people are without the necessary means to repair this waste, and yet the masses are very anxious to have public schools established. The American Union Commission co-operating with them, is aiding in the educational work in three ways.

1. It has opened some few schools for the poor, which it maintains at its own expense. Two such were sustained in Richmond last spring and summer, the Clergy giving the Commission the use of their lecture rooms for the purpose. [*See Mr. Chase's Report Post.*] The military authorities have now given us several fine buildings formerly belonging to the late confederacy. Our schools have been re-opened here and the frequent declaration that the poor whites have no desire to learn is sufficiently refuted by the fact that over a hundred children applied for admission before the teacher was on the ground to open the school.

2. It commissions first class teachers who desire to make the South their home, and engage in teaching there. These go out to organize schools and academies in places where such assistance is desired by the people. In such cases it does not maintain the schools, but renders the people such temporary assistance as is necessary to their maintenance.

3. It is co-operating with the free school party of the South in establishing permanent systems of public education. It has for this purpose united with them in obtaining from the military authorities the release and repair of public school buildings, has procured and commissioned, at the request of the civil authorities, two young men, graduates and teachers of experience, who have been appointed principals of the leading public schools of Nashville; has sent another at Gov. Brownlow's request to re-open the Academy at Knoxville, and others to less important points in Tennessee. It has sent into North Carolina one of the late instructors of Yale College, to whom Gov. Holden has promised every facility in reviving the schools and aiding the educational interest of that State; and it is now in correspondence with the State or local authorities in Arkansas, Tennessee, Virginia, North Carolina and Georgia, all of whom welcome our co-operation in this matter. In all these cases the schools are established in co-operation with the people, in buildings obtained from them, or with their sanction, and in every instance they are partially, in some cases, entirely supported by the community.

Observations.—The American Union Commission is National in its character, comprising branches organized not only in the principal cities of the North, but also in several of the Southern States. Though undenominational, it is Christian in its spirit and purposes, and proffers its co-operation and assistance in the work of evangelization to all the different denominations alike. It is catholic in its benefactions, recognizing no distinctions of caste or color, proffering its assistance to all men upon the score of a common humanity alone. Nevertheless, it carefully avoids the duplication of charities and conflict of organizations, by maintaining a cordial understanding and co-operation with the various societies organized for the special benefit of the colored people. Neither political nor sectional in its aims, it is nevertheless composed exclusively of men of recognized loyalty and fidelity to freedom. Its purpose is not to aid in restoring the old order of things which the war has swept away, but to co-operate with all who are now sincerely seeking the restoration of the Union, in re-establishing it upon the basis of universal freedom, education, industry, and Christian morality.

This work is one not only of charity, but of patriotism. We have but one country. In the welfare of every part of America, all Americans possess an equal interest. Especially is it clear even to the least thoughtful that popular education is essential to the perpetuity of popular government. We appeal then to all Americans to unite in this work of civil and social restoration. We ask the clergy, who have so well instructed their people in the duty of patriotic self sacrifice, to instruct them in the no less imperative duty of patriotic beneficence. We urge the women of America to continue, in behalf of their destitute countrymen, the labors which have so abundantly provided for the soldier. And we especially call upon the Churches, which gave us so generously the means to provide for the temporal wants of the refugees, to give us also the means to carry on this other and more important work.

REV. JOS. P. THOMPSON, D. D., Pres.
REV. LYMAN ABBOTT, General Secretary.
REV. GEO. J. MINGINS, D. D., Financial Secretary.
H. M. PIERCE, L. L. D., Recording Secretary.
GEO. W. LANE, ESQ. Chairman Executive Committee.
Hon. MARTIN BRIMMER, Chairman Ex. Com. of N. E. Branch, Boston.
SAML. C. MERRICK, ESQ., Pres. of Penn. Branch, Philadelphia.
G. S. GRIFFITHS, ESQ., Pres. of Maryland Branch, Baltimore.
COL. C. G. HAMMOND, Pres. of N. W. Branch, Chicago.
HON. E. ROOT, Pres. of Tenn. Branch, Nashville.
HORACE L. KENT, ESQ., Pres. of Richmond Branch, Virginia.

REPORTS AND CORRESPONDENCE.

RICHMOND.

EXTRACTS FROM C. T. CHASE'S REPORT.

"Send five hundred barrels flour for the starving poor of Richmond," telegraphed Rev. Mr. Williams, the agent of the Christian Commission, to Mr. Stuart. The dispatch was forwarded to Dr. Thompson, our President, who telegraphed me at Washington: "We send five hundred barrels flour to Richmond. Go with it and report." It was of the best Georgetown brands. Secretary Stanton ordered the transportation, and the little steamer *John S. Ide*, Wilson, master, brought it here. In order to prevent imposition and secure economy, the city was divided into twelve districts, and an inspector appointed, with moderate pay, in each. These gentlemen were residents of the city, and said to be loyal. Several of them had suffered incarceration in Libby and Castle Thunder, while all were believed to be well qualified for their work. They did it well, observing closely the instructions, which were given to them. These were to make a personal inspection in their respective districts, to issue orders for supplies to such as were needy and deserving, to avoid giving to the well, and to such as had means or wealthy friends, and especially to note the circumstances of such as had been loyal throughout the rebellion and report them to me. The result of this plan of inspection was that impostors were shut out. The truly needy of either color who had no one to stand up and speak for them, the feeble who could not endure the crowd at the United States Commissary's office, and those whom the "relief visitors" had neglected or refused, because of their known Unionism, were sought out. To such the substantial aid which we were enabled to give, was truly a God-send, and has often been received with tears and touching expressions of gratitude toward their Northern friends.

Who were Relieved.—"It may perhaps, give a clearer idea of the persons relieved, and the circumstances under which the relief was given, by noting the remarks on the inspector's tickets. Here are a few, which represent thousands:

A. B.—"An honest German woman; lives in hovel; husband sick with consumption six years; sells pies in the camp; has no stove; cooks on her neighbors'; has nothing now to live upon."

Aunt Cloe.—"A very worthy colored woman, 75 years old; master turned her off; makes a little by washing; hasn't asked anything of the government. Says government set her free; thinks she ought to support herself now."

Mrs. J.—"A widow, sick; has eight children; nothing to eat; no means; can't get doctor; none of them will come unless they are paid."

Mrs. A.—"Lives five miles on Fredericksburgh Railroad; husband crippled; five children; two sick; a poor woman; no means; works at hoeing corn or anything; thinks it honorable to work and glad to get it to do."

There were some grand spirits who never bowed before the fire of secession even in Richmond. A few of these were wealthy, but many became much reduced and have been objects of our especial care. Let us turn again to the inspector's tickets, briefly:

Mrs. D.—"Five brothers in the Union army; three other relatives in the United States service; daughters took care of sick Union prisoners; 10 in family; no means. Husband ran off to avoid conscription; would'nt fight, he said, against the old flag."

Mrs. T.—"Widow; kept boarders; would'nt illuminate when the city was illuminated because she could not rejoice over the downfall of her country."

Mrs. C.—"Threw out the old flag when the Yankees came in, which she had kept hid in her house."

Mrs. L.—"Secreted Union men at the peril of her liberty and life; no means now."

Could you know the sad tale of uncomplaining suffering which attaches to such words through such times as they have seen, you would admire the humblest of this noble band. Let it not be forgotten that a cold winter will find them out of food—out of fuel and clothing, if not out of house and home. I cannot speak of them as I ought, to give you a clear idea of their situation. It seems like speaking of the affairs of one's own household."

Who were Denied.—" Some came dressed in silks and furs, set off with jewelry, still clinging to their *effete* aristocracy. When they demanded assistance, we advised them to sell their jewelry. When they insisted that "you have taken away our property (slaves) who used to support us, and now you are bound to feed us," we replied, "we don't issue on that basis," and never did in any instance. Some came who admitted that they owned houses and lands, and others who had husbands in good health, and yet begged with an effrontery unknown to us before. To such we gave gratuitous information on the modes of raising money on real estate, or the price paid per thousand for clearing bricks among the ruins.

Soup-House.—" On learning that no use was made by the army of a large quantity of fresh beef, suitable for soup, and that also a quantity of confiscated rice could be had for the purpose, we started a soup-house, and issued daily, for three months, about 700 rations of rich, delicious soup, at a cost of less than a cent a ration. Very few who received soup obtained any other aid. Of course, a certain portion of society "didn't want soup," and we never found it necessary to cater to their tastes. There were enough poor, worthy people, white and colored, glad to get it. When mothers walked a mile and a half through the broiling hot, midday sun to get a few quarts of soup, you may know there was need of it in the household. Seventy-five thousand rations of soup were thus dispensed.

The Children and the Schools.—" The Freedmen's societies, while we were disbursing food to the hungry without distinction as to color, started several schools for the colored children, and gathered in large numbers who had hitherto been deprived of education. There was a section of the city known as Oregon Hill, where the old flag is said to have been kept floating longer than on any other spot in Virginia, and whose inhabitants claim *never to have been out of the Union.* The children had no schools, and hundreds were growing up in ignorance. An application came through Rev. Mr. McCarty, Baptist clergyman, to start a school in his church. It was accepted, and soon another started in the Methodist church near by. They increased rapidly; four teachers were employed, H. W. Harvey, graduate of New York State Normal School, as principal in the boys', and T. G. Wright, M. D., as principal in the girls' school, with two lady assistants, who resided in Richmond. They were supplied with books by the kind offices of Miss L. M. Thropp, who has a flourishing select school in Philadelphia. Another fine donation of books has been received of Messrs. Barnes & Burr, of New York. No charge was made for tuition."

Garden Seeds—Agricultural Implements.—" No expenditure by the commission has been more highly beneficial than the purchase of garden seeds for gratuitous distribution. We put them up in small packages and gave them out to persons having small farms to cultivate, thus affording the means of making a living to very many, and giving a renewal of good seed for their surrounding neighborhoods. Over 8000 papers have been distributed to applicants from all parts of the State. The released prisoners, as they laid on the ground in the square, often came round for meals and took home packages of seeds. They would sit in the front of the tent and talk of the war, denouncing it as "the rich man's war, but the poor man's fight," and not unfrequently express their honest love for the old flag above them, saying, "When I go to war again I shall go in under them Stars and Stripes." These men are yet to be the best citizens who have been engaged in the rebellion.

"The utter destruction of the country for many miles around the city has no precedence, except where the tread of armed men has been. We issued to small farmers in this region, plows, spades, shovels, &c., to the number of 150, having about as many more on hand. Thus many have been enabled to start again, and may, some day, repay this timely assistance afforded them.

The Fourth of July at our Tent.—" By special request of the citizens, the military authorities had permitted us to pitch our tent in the Capitol-square, at once the most beautiful and comfortable spot in Richmond. A photographer came on the afternoon of the Fourth to "take it." This attracted a small crowd. Soon many of our new friends and acquaintances joined it. We commenced distributing papers, thinking they would go away. This only attracted more. Then we read Whittier's poem of her, "the bravest of all in Fredericktown," and the Declaration of Independence. They gave in hearty response three cheers for the Stars and Stripes, *which always float over our tent,*

This impromptu demonstration was indeed a novelty. For four long years none who loved their country's flag had been permitted to see it floating there—and never before had the colored people enjoyed the privilege of the park on Freedom's birthday. They were largely represented at that gathering.

Virginia's Future.—"There are indications of a return to sanity, and of accepting the new order of things, which has uprooted their social life. Young men have gone out from their pleasant city mansions, and taken their places on the abandoned farms and gone faithfully to work. Young women, too, whose ancestry are among the revered of the nation are asking for employment. Often as they came for supplies, they have begged for work—"something—anything to do." "Give me that scoop," said one, "I'll shovel flour for you. I'm ashamed to beg; but I can't help it now; my support is gone." The returning soldiers, it is said, have generally applied themselves to some honest calling. All this is an earnest of better things.

"Those who own lands, or mines, or mill seats, will sell, often at low rates. Through the war the old barrier *exclusiveness* has been shaken and will be broken down. Capital and men from abroad are invited to come and resuscitate the waste places and develop the untouched wealth of the State. Thought is freer and speech is free. Truth and error will now contend side by side. The result cannot be doubtful. A new era of progress is at hand. If the public affairs of the State be wisely administered, and the property-holders act discreetly toward the laborers there need be no doubt of brighter days, higher intelligence, and truer prosperity arising in Virginia than ever prevailed in her borders.

What is Needed.—"But there is yet to be done in and for Virginia no small work by those who are the friends of true advancement and a nobler nationality. Just now there are thousands of poor who must receive assistance in food and clothing, or they will suffer from the cold and starvation during the coming winter.

"The plain people of the South are friendly to the National Union when left to themselves, they have been and will be so in future. But they are poor, very poor now, and need the friendly hand extended to them. They are ready and glad to take the hand of true philanthropy and follow its guidance. The rich can take care of themselves. Garden seeds are needed to plant a hundred thousand garden patches; for, to use a common remark among them, "Good seed ran out under the Confederacy." Good teachers and high-minded Christian ministers have a rich and wide field here to enter upon. If they come in the right spirit they will win their way and be a blessing."

C. THURSTON CHASE.

RICHMOND, Va., Aug. 31, 1865.

Free Schools.—The schools referred to in this report could not be carried on permanently in the lecture rooms of churches. And as soon as vacation and a little relief from the pressing importunities of the destitute gave Mr. Chase the leisure, he began to look about for appropriate buildings in which to re-open the schools in the fall. To secure these was a matter of no little difficulty. Nearly one-third of the city having been destroyed by fire, while the population of the city was greatly increased by the numbers who flocked to it from the surrounding country, it was almost impossible to secure, even at exorbitant rents, a room to sleep in, much less buildings adequate to the work which the Commission had undertaken. This the indefatigable energy of Mr. Chase accomplished—*rent free.* But we will let him tell his story in in his own words, merely premising that we quote, not from official reports, but from private letters not written for publication.

"Work has won.—I have this day, (Aug. 25th), taken possession, under orders from Maj. Gen. Turner, of the Confederate Naval Laboratory and Arsenal. These buildings are on Oregon Hill, and consist of two framed, each 20 x 35 ft., one framed, 20 x 75 ft., one brick, 22 x 35 ft., one ditto, 30 x 65 ft., and one ditto, 15 ft. square, each one story. The wooden buildings are ceiled inside and pretty well lighted, adapted to school rooms and teachers' quarters. The brick are also one story, high ceilings, not well lighted, all slate roofed. They are by far the best Confederate buildings I have ever seen in the South. There is also a stable attached. The yard surrounding is well graveled. There is a good well in the grounds. All are finely enclosed. * * * *

"*Sep. 22nd.*—Following up my propensity to get things without paying for them! I have succeeded in securing a lot of settees, which, with a few benches I have bought, and a few more confiscated, will probably make enough for our Laboratory schools. It looks now as though we should get a good outfit for $100. which in ordinary way would cost $500 or more. * * * Yesterday, got 1000 ft. of lumber *gratis*, and shall at once use it in preparing the teachers' rooms. * * * I have 25 of the desks from the rebel halls of Congress. Have bought no lumber. tore down the yard-fence to get it. * * * *Oct. 9th*, I opened the schools finally at nine o'clock by reading the 15th Chap. of John, and repeating the Lord's Prayer in concert with the school. About a hundred and fifty girls and boys were present. As I commenced registering their names, Mr. Washburne came in. I have telegraphed to Miss Kate Thropp, of Philadelphia, of whom you are already informed, to come on immediately. We shall want three lady teachers in the Laboratory schools. * * * The weather is fine, and the prospect for our work never looked fairer.

"C. THURSTON CHASE."

On the 1st of October, Mr. Andrew Washburne, an experienced teacher from Mass., formerly principal of a Normal school in that State, was engaged to go to Richmond to superintend the educational work of the Commission. On the 19th, ten days after the opening of the school, he writes reporting that the one school has grown into three; that the attendance has increased to 235; that he is compelled to refuse admission to any more, as the rooms are already full; and, that two applications have been made to him to open additional free schools in different parts of the city. These facts sufficiently demonstrate the falsity of the oft repeated statement, that the children of the poorer classes of the non-slaveholding whites of the South, have no desire to learn. They are exceedingly eager for instruction.

A Committee, consisting of Messrs. Rev. Leonard, W. Bacon, D. D., of New Haven, and Christopher R. Robert, Esq., of New York, have now gone to Richmond for the purpose of consulting with leading citizens there, in respect to the adoption of some system of co-operation in promoting the cause of popular education in the city and the State. We hope to have their report in time to append to this pamphlet.

TENNESSEE.

ABSTRACT OF HON. E. ROOT'S REPORTS.

Refugees.—"The Nashville Refugee Aid Society was organized March 17th, 1864, and subsequently by vote, became a branch of the American Union Commission. There has also been a very efficient ladies' society, entitled "The Ladies' Union Aid Society," which, though maintaining a separate organization, has acted as an auxiliary. Most of our distributions of clothing and provisions for the sick in Refugee Hospitals, have been made through this branch.

"It is estimated that the receipts in cash and supplies up to date, (June, 1865), will not fall short of $25,000, and that the whole number assisted, will not fall short of 20,000. Last year, (1864), the Society employed Mr. R. E. Farwell to conduct a refugee farm in the vicinity of Nashville. It furnished a home for about a hundred and twenty-five, mostly women and children.

"A day school and Sunday shool was organized for the children, about forty of whom attended regularly.—*The fathers of these children were for the most part soldiers in the Union Army.* The labor on the farm was performed entirely by refugees, and the products went for their sustenance.

Their estimated value was about $4,000. In March last, by request of Maj. Gen. Thomas, I sent supplies to the destitute families in Decatur, Alabama, for which I drew on Mr. Odiorne, of Cincinnati, (the Western Secretary of the Union Commission.)

Education.—"It is to be hoped that the calls for relief among refugees will cease in a few months, but the work of the Union Commission will not then be finished. If I understand correctly the object of its organization, the question presents itself: What plan of benevolence will best secure the greatest amount of good to the Southern States, just emerging from a state of anarchy, into a new order of social life? I will briefly indicate what, in my judgment, such a plan should be —The Southern States never had a public school system. Their peculiar system of labor forbade it. They had private schools which afforded instruction to the few, while the many were compelled to grow up and remain in ignorance. The late rebellion in the main grew out of this fact. This must be changed. The intellectual and moral character of the Southern people can be elevated and sustained only through the medium of common schools, accessible to all classes—white and colored—and by faithful Christian teaching from the pulpit. Tennessee will establish her schools for white and colored pupils. These schools will need well qualified teachers, and the Union Commission can render valuable assistance in supplying the schools with such teachers. Some pecuniary aid may also be required in sustaining the teachers in these schools for a short time, which it may be well for the Commission to render."

SCHOOLS ESTABLISHED IN TENNESSEE.

Nashville.—The suggestions of this report in respect to schools have been carried out. In the spring of 1865 there were no free schools in Nashville. The school buildings were still occupied as hospitals by the military. In May a committee visited Washington to urge the surrender of the buildings to their proper purpose. It was done. At the request of the city educational authorities, two young men were sent out by the Commission, especially selected by a committee of Yale College, of which they were graduates, to take charge, the one of the classical department of the High School, the other of the principal public school of the city. The latter, Mr. Ware, writes on the 25th of September:—

"I reached this city in safety on the evening of Saturday, the 9th inst. I found myself on my arrival appointed to the Principalship of the Howard School—the largest public school in the city. The house is a very good one, much better than I expected to find South. It will accommodate 800, and require 15 teachers. The position is very difficult and responsible. There have been no public schools here for four years, and the houses have been used as hospitals. The task of bringing order out of the chaotic mass which came together last Monday, was no small one; but we have been at it a week, and to day there was a collection of children which looked and acted quite like a school.

"There is beginning to be a good deal of interest here in the subject of education. The State Teachers' Association, a new organization, held its services in the State House, last week, Thursday and Friday. Though the numbers were not large yet the spirit was good. I have had the pleasure of listening to a bill creating a fine school system for the Sate, which is soon to be introduced into the legislature. It is a very liberal bill, giving six months education to all children *black and white;* and should it pass, as there is reason to hope it will, it will put Tennessee on a par with any of her sister States in educational advantages. The great trouble for the present will be a want of competent teachers. I think many must come from the North.

"Allow me to give you a simple sketch of the history and present condition of the public schools of Nashville. In 1854, a house was erected here for free school purposes, and Mr. J. F. Pearl, formerly Superintendent of Public Schools in Natchez, Miss., then Superintendent of Public Schools, Memphis, Tenn, was invited to come here and organize a system of public schools. In December of that year he came, and in February, 1855, the school was commenced. That house the Hume Building, was soon full, and others were erected, till there were four in all,—the Hume, Hynes, Trimble, and Howard. Of these, the Howard is the largest and the best planned. Under Mr. Pearl's management, the schools went on very prosperously till the war broke out. In July, 1861, Mr. Pearl was warned away from Nashville by the Vigilance Committee, and went North. The schools continued under rebel management something less than a year and then closed. The houses have been used by the Government as hospitals. After this interregnum of four years we are just getting under way again. Of course, all the organizing and grading has to be done over again. I can assure you it is no small task.

"Before the war there were about twenty-two hundred children in the schools. There are not quite as many as that now, but they are coming in very rapidly. At the Howard Building I have about six hundred and fifty, with room for about one hundred more. We are having, so far, very good success, and hope we shall continue to do so. We are here at the State Capital, and are every way "a city set on a hill." I hope we shall be able to give a good light to guide the State onward and upward in the good cause of popular education."

Knoxville.—In August last, we received from Gov. Brownlow a letter containing the following extract:—

"We have a brick academy, in East Knoxville, 40 x 60 ft., two stories high. The most of the building was erected by me, by subscription, for a high school and for religious worship. It would be the very place for Mr. Adams of whom you spoke, to start in, but it is occupied by our forces as a military prison, and mechanics estimate that it will require $3,000 to put it in order. I understand the military intend to surrender it soon. * * * I would assist Mr. Adams in getting up a free school there, and introducing himself for future usefulness, if we had the building."

Immediate application was made to the military authorities for assistance in putting this academy in order. It was granted. Mr. Adams having been already commissioned to act as agent in Georgia, Mr. John K. Payne, another graduate, was sent thither instead. He has opened the academy successfully; writes, that his school is nearly self-supporting, and probably will be entirely so; that he commenced with thirty pupils, and that the number promises to double in a week or two. He has already written to us to send out three other teachers to East Tennessee. One of these is already on the way. In Mr. Payne's last letter, 6th October, he writes:

"The Commission will not be called on for any repairs for my academy, as the public funds have proved sufficient, and the Trustees have turned over to me the current rent of a dwelling-house attached to the academy (all belongs to the State), for further repairs. My school is very pleasant and promising; thirty-four pupils this week and six more promised for next week. Most of these will pay $3 per month tuition. Th s is the only school-house to accommodate about 400 boys who live in Knoxville. I am visiting and getting acquainted, and can probably enlarge my school so as to justify two teachers."

More Schools Wanted.—On the 16th of October he writes again:

"Rev. Samuel Sawyer, lately of Knoxville, now preaching at Rogersville, whence he was driven by the rebels three years ago, informed me two weeks ago, that a first-rate teacher was needed there, and he mentioned an adjoining village suitable for commencing a school. Jacksboro has been represented to me as a good place, and there is room for another school in Blount Co., which by the way is one of the best educational counties in the State. I have talked with men who attend Court here, from every quarter and of every station in life, and my general impression is that an enterprising man could succeed in any of the county towns, especially those I have named."

Mr. W. B. Davenport, of Yale College, was sent out in September, at the request of Rev. M. Lamar, a Presbyterian Clergyman of Marysville, East Tennessee, to open a school there. On arriving there, he was heartily welcomed by the people. He writes under date of 3rd October:

"On the 25th I commenced my labors with nearly thirty wild urchins, who had hardly attended school for three and a half years. I brought much zeal to the work, but found the stock had to be replenished every day. The school-house is built of logs, 20 ft. long, 16 ft. broad, seats are boards on pins in the form of a T, without vestige of backs; here I preside with all the dignity I can summon. As yet all has gone smoothly. I have endeavored to maintain order without the whip, a thing never before attempted in this region. I think I shall succeed. I wrote to Judge Root in respect to the need of wheat seed for planting, and I think he may have written you.

"Here they plant wheat the second week in October, the crop this Spring was very small, and they have not enough to plant, and can hardly buy any at any price. As a general thing the people are kind, generous, and hospitable. No one could be more so, but their means are small—their houses are small. No Union man can be found who has not lost more or less of stock.

"*For three years they have had to depend on Rebels for teachers altogether.*"

The spirit of the people of East Tennessee and their great anxiety to secure the blessings of popular education, are strikingly illustrated by the following extract, clipped from the recent address to his constituency, by Geo. E. Grisham, Esq., a candidate for the Tennessee legislature:

"Should it be your pleasure to elect me, fellow citizens, the first and greatest question which shall engage my attention will be that of education. Upon this subject I may be considered an enthusiast. But the importance attaching thereto should demand the most serious consideration and zeal of our law-making and public representatives. In my humble judgment, there is no question which is of greater or more vital interest to our country. In the palmiest days of our State, our system of education was never what it ought to have been. Let us look at the Northern States of our Union, and behold the contrast! For instance, take a regiment of soldiers from a Northern State, and as a general rule, you will find that at least nine-tenths of the members can read and write. Take one of our Tennessee regiments, and behold how sad has been the neglect of men, who have hitherto had the control and management of our State affairs. The 'Township System' of education in the North has worked wonders in the diffusion of useful knowledge among the masses. Here, we have been ground down by the heel of a petty aristocracy, who cared not for the common people. But, thanks to a benign Providence, the day of their destiny is over; and, to day, the eagle of liberty perches upon the banner of a free and independent Republic. Now can we begin to lift our eyes and behold, through the glorious sun-light of God's blessings, the handwriting on the wall—'Progress—Refinement—Education—Liberty—Success!' Fellow Citizens, above all things else, we need the intellectual and moral training of our youth, which, for four dreadful years of bloodshed and carnage, have been almost entirely neglected. The condition of our country, in this respect, is a stigma upon our fair fame as a people—a people whose loyalty has been that of undying devotion."

Fellow Citizens, this is an unconscious appeal to you. What answer do you make to it? Will you, who have always enjoyed the blessings of a free education, extend your aid to such noble spirits, endeavouring to secure to their children henceforth those privileges which in the past have been denied them?

GEORGIA.

Physical Destitution.—In some parts of Georgia the prospects are very encouraging—the crops, though small in quantity, are good; industry is reviving and trade is re-commencing. But in other localities the destitution is very great; and the most favored portions of the State only have enough for their own support. Nowhere is there surplus sufficient to meet the wants of the more destitute neighborhoods. The track of Sherman's army is a scene of desolation, especially between Chattanooga and Atlanta, and in the region immediately about Savannah. Having received both through the military authorities at Macon and Atlanta, and from the citizens of Savannah, a strong representation of their necessitous condition, two agents were sent to explore and report the facts. Hon. E. Root, of Nashville, was directed to visit Atlanta from the North, and Mr. E. B. Adams, a few weeks later, was sent to Savannah, with directions to explore the State from that point, traversing especially the track of Sherman's army, and thus reaching Atlanta from the East. Mr. Root was provided by Government with a special train for the purpose. In his report, dated 4th September, he writes:

"I have recently made a journey through Northern Georgia and Alabama, and Eastern Tennessee. Houses, fences, cattle, horses, sheep, hogs and chickens, have almost entirely disappeared, and the women and children and few remaining men are in a state of great destitution. The villages between Chattanooga and Atlanta are in ruins, and I do not remember seeing a smile on any human face in any place there is between those two points. Through that whole distance, *I did not see as much food growing for man or beast as can be found on a respectable Northern farm.* In Southern Tennessee and Northern Alabama, the condition is much the same. In almost every house that is left standing, want and famine are the principal inmates. This you can see in the faces of the women and children. Corn meal is their principal food, and of this the daily allowance is small. Many have not had a taste of meat of any kind for months. Most of those who have land have not means of cultivating it. The war has left them with nothing to work with. * * * In East Tennessee the condition of things was very different. There I saw respectable farms under cultivation with comparatively good crops."

This statement is abundantly confirmed by Mr. Adams. He shall tell his story in his own words. We only regret that we have not space for the publication of his letters in full. They bear date, September 19th, 23rd, 27th, and October 2nd, 11th, and 20th:

Savannah.—"There is frightful destitution here. It is partially met by the Home Relief Fund, which obtains its resources from an amount of rice which Gen. Sherman captured here. This enables the city to distribute the following rations to adults and one-half of the same to children, viz.:—2 lbs. rice, 3 lbs. flour, and 1 lb. meal for two week's subsistence. But by the middle of November this and its source will be altogether consumed; and furthermore, the people, according to the most reliable information, cannot support their poor. When this Home Relief Fund began its work it canvassed the city, put on its books only those who "could not live" without,—helpless widows, the infirm, etc.—excluding all healthy males; all females who had "healthy husbands," or were themselves young and healthy. The number on the books is about seven hundred families, averaging three grown persons each; two children counting as one adult, excluding a hundred and forty-nine refugee families, which the city hopes will be supported by the government. This arrangement and some of the men who are engaged in this work are at our service whenever I think it best to introduce supplies. I can have storage and office rooms free of expense.

Two Cases of Destitution.—"I saw a family last Monday, consisting of a man who had an amputated yet unhealed arm, suffering from typhoid fever, a wife, and three small children, one of whom has also the typhoid fever. This family lives in a very poor old hut, possesses only what clothing they have on their backs. The two sick ones were stretched out on the floor with nothing but an old army blanket underneath. They subsist entirely on the small ration given by the Home Fund. This is only one out of hundreds similar. Now what are such persons going to do during the coming winter. * * * *

"There are very many wretched beings about the bye-ways of the city, who have nothing scarcely to cover them. So, too, the country about is filled with them, though they are fast coming to the city. I met, a few days since, a woman, who, with a large family of children, had just come in. She reports that two men came to her garden, picked off the green ears of corn, stole her pig, and took away everything she had, leaving her utterly destitute of winter support These men, probably, were in equally destitute circumstances, and were stealing to bring into market and exchange for the necessities of life. She, with her family, had walked about twenty miles to get here. * * * *

"My little observation in the adjacent towns has afforded me a *slight* insight to great destitution. The people contrive to get something to eat by hunting and fishing, but appear altogether destitute of a comfortable lodging. Every one speaks of terrible suffering in the adjoining counties. *They tell of naked human beings curling down by the side of their once prosperous and comfortable homes, now reduced to nothing save the roots of an old brick chimney*; or, sleeping in sheds sometimes, and eating only what they can beg, steal, or pick up. This is report, coming, however, from authentic sources. * * * The spirit of the people appears good. They are willing to accept the condition they are in as a necessary result of the war, and feel grateful for any marks of sympathy or even for anticipated assistance.

"The city is thoroughly destitute of all mechanical industry. One wheat-grinding mill and an iron foundry on a small scale, is all there is of that class of business. Not one chair, turner, pail, tub, cloth, or paper factory. One man is here to day, from the North I suppose, purchasing rags, old cotton, paper, etc., for the merely nominal price of a quarter to half a cent per pound, which are worth at the North from three to ten cents. Water privileges are excellent here, I am told, and why should not these things be manufactured here.

Education.—"I hear various and contradictory reports in regard to the educational status of Georgia. One class of men say that Georgia is one hundred years behind in education. Another say Georgia is a fairly educated State, she stands on an equal footing with Mass. or Conn. My opinion is that both are partially correct. The aristocrats are fairly educated. But the "poor whites" the "Crackers" are sadly deficient. In Clinch Co., as the Provost Marshall, who administered to her inhabitants the oath, says, eighty out of a hundred can neither read nor write. This is a fact. How, now, can they be educated?"

On the 20th day of October, Mr. Adams having returned from a tour of Central Georgia, in which he visited Milledgeville, Augusta, Macon, Atlanta, and other points, writes a full report of his journey. In the course of this trip he had interviews both with leading men of the State and with officers of the Freedmen's Bureau.

"Yours of September 25th and 30th, and October 3rd and 10th, together with Mr. Allan's of the 7th October, announcing the shipment of clothing, are at hand. Having just arrived in this city, I have not examined the clothing—shall give my attention to that matter immediately. Without doubt, I can get free transportation for the quantity destined for Athens. It will be very timely both here and there. * * * *

Agricultural Wants.—"The charity that would be most acceptable and effectual to the upper portion of the State, is, a distribution of seeds and agricultural implements. I learn that the counties of Dade, Catoosa, Whitfield, Gordon, Cass, Cobb, Fulton, Dekalb, and Clayton, were literally swept, and are now utterly destitute (*i. e.* in the case of a majority of the families), of things of this kind. * * * *

"In *Macon* there is much personal destitution and distress. There are five hundred helpless widows, and each widow has, upon the average, two children each, making in all one thousand children. These fifteen hundred white people are dependent upon the charity of the city. The negroes here are in a frightful state of want and suffering. The city does nothing for them but to bury them when dead. The number thus interred in Macon, averages seventy-five to a hundred weekly. Ten were picked up dead in the streets last week. Such is the mortality and suffering among these poor people, in spite of what is done for them by the Bureau. Supplies of food are furnish d by Government to the worst cases. There are eight colored schools in Macon, superintended by the Rev. Mr. Roberts. * * * *

"The great majority of the white children, there being about six hundred old enough for school, are without its privileges. There are several private schools there, but few, comparatively, of the poor orphans can attend. I conversed with several prominent men in regard to the education of these. They are anxious for it, and willing to have free schools opened. The Mayor favors the teaching of these poor children,—says the city will co-operate and assist a good deal. I would respectfully suggest that we make the following proposition to the Mayor and Aldermen of Macon—viz., to procure, free of expense to the city, two male teachers for one year, who shall open two primary free schools, provided that the city furnish suitable buildings and assistant lady teachers; schools to begin January 1st, 1866. * * *

Atlanta.—"There are many in Atlanta who have no shelter of any kind, but sleep where night overtakes them,—every old dilapidated freight-car is converted into a dwelling-house. Every rag of canvas or old tent deserted by the soldiers, is made a home for families,—every old shed is occupied. Food is a very costly article, and in many cases insufficient. Yet the Mayor says, 'We will try and get along; if you can assist us to schools you will do the present generation great good. The military power grants rations to the poor and destitute whom I recommend.' 'We who have a little will also do something,' says another. * * There are one or two private schools there. But there are five hundred children who have no school privileges. A good share of these would gladly attend a charitable school."

NORTH CAROLINA.

. In this State there was before the war a strong interest in the cause of popular education. There was a large school fund. And, notwithstanding the difficulties in the way of establishing a system of public schools, very considerable progress had been made in that direction. Even during the war, owing largely to the efforts of C. H. Wiley, Esq., the Superintendent of Public Instruction, the schools were continued. But the close of the Confederacy brought them to a close. The funds were nearly all lost in the universal wreck. And, though the people are very anxious to have free schools re-established, there appears to be little prospect that they will be able to provide for the wants of their State, by either contributions or taxation. Rev. Fiske P. Brewer, formerly one of the instructors of the scientific department of Yale College, has gone into North Carolina, under the auspices of this Commission, to aid in re-establishing public schools in that State. He is warmly welcomed by Gov. Holden, who writes to him: "I will particularly lend all the aid in my power to the great and permanent cause of education;" and, by Mr. Wiley, who writes: "If we expect to remain a free and civilized people, we must educate our children."

From Mr. Brewer's letters we make some extracts. They bear date the last of September and the first of October:

An Interview with Gov. Holden.—"I called on Gov. Holden last night, at his house, by invitation. He says, 'The people are as poor as they can be. In the Eastern portions of the State, in Wilmington, and Newbern especially, which have been longest in the National possession, there has been the greatest revival of industry, and there the people might do something for the support of free schools. In this city, in Hillsboro, Greensboro, and Charlotte, all important centres, they could hardly do anything at present; but instruction for the poor is much needed.' He is for immigration and everything that would favor it, as is also every one that I met. He says the Northern people must come down here, as they go into the Western States, and bring their free schools with them.' " * * *

Schools in Raleigh.—"I have been making personal explorations about this city, and am convinced that a school which will admit children free is a great desideratum. My estimate is that there are over five hundred schoolable children here, and not over two hundred and twenty-five in school. At a house where I was this morning, the girl, fourteen years old, has just left off school because they could not afford the reduced rate of two dollars a month, which the teacher had consented to receive. 'We are all pressed down,' said the mother, by way of apology. 'I wish you would start a school here,' said the girl, 'I'd like to begin next week.' At another house I asked the girl, of about the same age, if it would be a good place in that neighborhood for a school. 'There are a heap of poor children here that would like to go if there was one where they could; I'd like to go myself.' * * * I have the promise of a building here in the city for our purposes. It was formerly a church, but for four years has contained army harnesses. It is too small for the highest utility, 34 x 42 ft. outside, and needs some cleaning, etc., but it is in the best possible location, in the heart of the city. I have offered the trustees fifty dollars for the use of it the coming year, and the offer has been accepted." * * *

A teacher, a graduate of Yale College, Mr. O. R. Burchard, of Binghampton, N. Y., has been sent on to open this school, which will doubtless be commenced before this report can be in print.

Beaufort.—"Last night I returned from a very instructive trip to Beaufort. I have learned the feeling of the people on free schools and education generally. Beaufort is a good position for an able teacher of boys. There is a good room in possession of the Freedmen's Bureau, which Capt. McSnell offered to turn over to us. I would recommend that the place be occupied by a first-class teacher, who will make himself some reputation by actual teaching, and then appeal to the town to support him at the head of a free school. There are in the city a hundred and fifty children of schoolable age, whose parents are, or think they are too poor to pay."

Wilmington.—"Wilmington has a population of 12,000. Number of children in school about five hundred—in some twenty schools. Usual tuition in good schools is $75 for nine months. Children too poor to attend school estimated at five hundred. The town included four school districts and had two schools. One of the buildings has been torn down during the war." * *

Mr. Brewer called upon the school committee, who welcomed him most cordially, and manifested an earnest desire to have a free school opened in the remaining building, the use of which they offered him for the purpose. Their statement, written at his request, give the facts very fully.

"We have in our district, which comprises two school districts, a very good school-house, capable of acommodating from one hundred to a hundred and twenty scholars.

"We will put this at your service. As the patrons of the former school were very poor, there is little to expect from them in the way of remuneration. We made our old school under the name of "Union Free School" entirely free, giving always the preference to the most needy.

"It is doubtful if you can rely upon any assistance. Yet there are many who would willingly assist did their means permit. The school-house is at your service to establish a free school for poor white children. And we will gladly avail ourselves of the assistance so kindly volunteered by your Commission. We have heretofore received from the State the quota of two districts, amounting to from $200 to $250 per annum. We do not think this annual amount will be discontinued, as every effort of our citizens will be excited to aid this object."

ARKANSAS.

The following report of Rev. J. H. Leard, formerly a Chaplain in the Union Army, gives an account of the condition and wants of the people of Arkansas.

Fort Smith, Ark., September 30th, 1865.

Rev. Lyman Abbott, Secretary American Union Commission:

"Dear Sir,—During the months of August and September I have been making investigations in regard to the destitution of the people of Arkansas. To accomplish this I have obtained the voluntary services of ten gentlemen living in as many different counties, besides several prominent officers and citizens, who have been and are now traveling over the State. I have visited Sebastian, Crawford, Franklin, Johnson, Yell, Hot Springs, Scott, Pelaski, Worchita, and Saline, embracing the larger portion of the State and following the war track. Having been in the State the last two years, and the most of the time serving the poor, I am familiar with their wants."

Destitution.—"The greatest desolation by the war and consequently the greatest destitution, are in the western, north-western, and eastern portions of the State. Though the interior and southern counties suffered much, yet compared with the other portions of the State they are in a good condition. A great part of what was known as the "Frontier District," during the war, is simply in ruins, marked by a desolation of the most saddening character. Towns, villages, and farm-houses are burnt to the ground, the chimneys still standing to remind the observer of the elegant mansion or cottage, and the once happy but now ruined family. Churches and school-houses have shared a like destruction. The farms are grown over with a luxuriant crop of weeds; the fences in many places burnt and the fields an open waste. The stock (where the army was) left alive has grown wild, and cannot easily be recognised by owners. Thousands of families who have been in exile are returning to meet this prospect. They come with nothing to start life anew, not even garden seeds.

"They are trying to get a little to eat and wear, and are moving into the smoke-houses and stables that have escaped the devouring flames, until they can do better. Many will haul with a poor ox-team, or cows yoked up, their bread from one to three hundred miles, and glad to get it even on such terms.

"But little grain has been raised in the western counties this year, but in the southern, corn is reported to be abundant and cheap. The colonies about the military stations raised a moderate crop of corn, but little more, however, than will supply themselves, as it is now clearly seen since the crop is gathered.

"It was thought during the early part of the season that the people might subsist themselves upon what they had raised, with what would be brought from a distance by merchants and others, but it is now evident that many, very many of the poor will suffer, unless the hand of benevolence supplies them. By the poor, we mean the aged, sick, cripples, the widows and orphans, whose name is legion.

"*Governor Murphy* writes to me as follows: "Every county in the State needs the work of the Commission, but especially Van Buren, Bard, Fulton, Madison, Leary, Newton, Carrol, and Marion. The people of those counties are starving both for material and intellectual aid. This field will richly repay cultivation. God bless the noble Union Commission. Its labors will produce a rich harvest.

"We will be under the necessity of calling on our Northern friends for help to keep the poor from starving."

Want of Clothing.—I intend to apprise them as soon as possible of the facts. Many that can subsist themselves cannot renew their clothing. There is but little money among the poor people, and no cotton scarcely cultivated. They can neither buy nor manufacture clothing in many cases, and must be supplied, or exposure and death will ensue. Not unfrequently, women and children walk to Fort Smith over roads of twenty to fifty miles, without a change of clothing, in search of food. and at *this time I have no supply on hand for them.* We must have vast quantities of clothing as soon as possible.

"*Will not the ladies enable us to meet this pressing want! Will they not organize their sewing societies this winter to relieve this frightful destitution!*

Education.—I have opened no schools yet, though the intellectual wants of the people are great, yet for months, or till another crop is raised, the great struggle will be for *life*. I am waiting for instuctions from the Commission on that subject; in the meantime laboring to create a living sentiment in favor of the free school system, which I hope will prevail at no very distant day in all the South. This is a great desideratum. I have met with no positive opposition to the Commission. The poor loyal people of Arkansas will receive it with gladness, and regard it as the work of love. No one can calculate the salutary moral influence it may exert as well as the material relief it may give. * * * *

Loyal Sufferers.—The broad belt of desolation through the State, as a general rule, marks the loyalty to the general government, as is evidenced by the historical fact that the ten thousand Union soldiers of this State were raised in this region. Here the "Bushmen" perpertrated their dark deed of cruelty upon the persons of loyal peope, the remaining of whom are the sufferers Many were brutally murdered, others exiled by the storm of persecution, their property laid waste, and now after the sufferings of the past, they return to the miseries of want.

"Will not the liberality that produced the Christian and Sanitary Commissions come to the relief of these sufferers of the nation?

"Respectfully submitted,

"J. H. LEARD,

"Agent A. U. C. for Arkansas."

New York City.

Mr. Geo. H. Allan, General Agent of the Commission, reports as follows concerning his work in this city:

"Fifteen hundred destitute Southern refugees have been aided in New York City, since January 1st, 1865. Most of these people had lost their all during Sherman's great march, and came to the North to avoid impending starvation. Hunger and exposure had reduced them to a deplorable condition. While crowded together in one of the barracks at the Battery, small-pox and measles broke out among them, and at one time, forty persons were suffering with these diseases.

"In April, by direction of the Commission, two "Homes for Refugees" were opened; one at the Battery, and the other in W. 24th Street, by which these people were rendered much more comfortable. Within a few weeks, four hundred persons were sent to the West, and an equal number found employment in the North and East. The remainder for the most part have returned to the South since the termination of the war. During the few days they were with us, they were provided with food, clothing, and medicine; also transportation to the interior.

"*Six thousand garments*, donated by the benevolent public, were distributed among them, and were received with gratitude. Many who had landed in this city in a state of despair, were thus rendered hopeful for the future.

"Education among these people was sadly deficient. Hardly one in ten could read or write. Their minds were filled with wonder and amazement at the sight of Northern activity and progress, and this lesson will not be lost upon them. Our late President was mourned by them sincerely, many of them voluntarily wearing the sable badge. I have never heard one of them speak of Mr. LINCOLN with disrespect.

"Many interesting incidents concerning the loyalty of these people came under my notice. I will mention a few:

"Rev. Mr. G———, of Georgia, brought letters from Union officers, certifying that he had helped them when sick and in prison. He had been wealthy, but had lost all, and fled with his family to the North. Kind friends aided us in giving them shelter while in this city, and Government gave them transportation to the West. In a few weeks we learned that Mr. G. had hired a steam saw-mill in Central Illinois, and was succeeding finely. He had established a Sabbath School in a destitute neighborhood, and had commenced regular meetings for Divine service.

"Mrs. T——, a Union woman of Charleston, also applied to us for assistance. She had resided in Charleston during the rebellion, and had supported herself by making bags, designed to be filled with sand, for use on the rebel fortifications. The remnants were thrown into a closet, and afterwards used by her in making shirts for Union prisoners. She also visited sick Union soldiers in the rebel hospitals, and gave them fruit and delicacies. Lieut. Fales, a Union officer, having been taken prisoner by the rebels, escaped and found a refuge in her house. Here he was taken down with yellow fever, but she nursed him, under a double peril, for weeks, with the tenderness of a mother; she saved his life, and finally aided his escape to his regiment. Lieut. F., who is now an editor in this city, narrated to me these facts, and Gen. Howard, on hearing of her noble conduct, immediately sent us an order for her transportation to Charleston.

"Mr. S.———, of Florida, a good Union man, sixty years of age, was treated with every indignity on account of his devotion to the old flag;—at last, the rebels burned his house, killed his stock, and took him out to a large tree near by to hang him. Adjusting the noose round his neck, and throwing the rope over a limb of the tree, they told him to 'hurrah for

Jeff. Davis.' '*Never*,' said he, '*If I am to die, I will die a Union man.*' Three times the miscreants suspended him by the neck, each time trying to force him to relinquish his Union sentiments. Finding him fixed in his determination, they cast him half dead into prison, whence, after two months captivity, he escaped. He was at our 'Home' nearly two weeks, but has since returned to the South. He was a member of the Methodist church, and his whole deportment was that of a consistent Christian.

"Mr. N———, a mechanic, from Charleston, stopped with his family a few days for rest at the 'Home.' As I gave him his tickets, food for his journey, and a little present in money, his wife burst into tears, and said, 'Thomas, when we were feeding that poor Yankee soldier in Charleston, I told you God would reward us, and now He is doing it.' For a few moments the scene was affecting, especially when her little daughter came in, wondering 'what mamma was crying for.' I afterwards learned from them, that Martin Beckman, an Illinois soldier, having made his escape from Andersonville, and reaching Charleston, in the disguise of a rebel soldier, had found an asylum at their house. They were poor, but Union loving people, and told him they would share their last crust with him. They provided for him for three weeks, and at a time when bread was worth $4 a loaf, and mechanics' wages but $7 per day. At the end of that time the soldier made his escape to his regiment."

"Mr C———, a Union man from Savannah, came North, wearing a white Southern coat. Some idle fellows on Broadway, hooted at him and called him a 'rebel.' He stopped, and told them he was a loyal man, and only wore the coat because he had no other. They still continued their insulting remarks, until finding argument useless, he thrashed one of them soundly, when the rest made off. He came and asked my advice; I told him to put the old coat into the stove, which he did. I then gave him a good suit of clothes and he had no further trouble. He finally settled in Wisconsin.

"Mrs. H———, of Columbia, S. C., came to our 'Home' with her three children. She was a loyal woman, but her husband was a rebel soldier, and refused to write to her. While he was away, she supported herself and children by sewing. Times were very hard. She fed and secreted Capt. Reeves and other Pennsylvania officers, and aided their escape. She was obliged to live mostly on corn meal, as prices were very high. For months beef was $3 per lb ; eggs, $5 per doz.; meal, 50 cts. per lb.; butter, $9 to $14 per lb.; coffee, $28 to $30 per lb.; bacon, $6 per lb.; sugar, $28 to $30 per lb.; calico, $20 per yard; cotton cloth, $8 to $12 per yard; flour, $400 per bbl. At this time she could only make $2 per day with her needle, and yet she helped Union prisoners. We assisted her, and sent her to her relatives, near Circleville, Ohio.

"Mr. M———, of S. C., a loyal man, proprietor of an iron foundry. Was worth $50,000 in 1860. Refused to cast shot and shell for the rebels, and his foundry was the only idle one in the State during the war. Of this I have abundant proof. All his property was destroyed during Sherman's march, by Union troops. He came North with his family. We gave them food and clothing, and sent them to Iron Mountain, Mo.

"Among others, we have assisted a niece of President Munroe, and also a grand-daughter of Peter Faneuil, who, a hundred years ago, presented the "Cradle of Liberty" to the Bostonians."

Numerous letters of gratitude have been received from those who for a time have tarried with us. Those who have settled in the West have commenced farming for themselves or have gone to work on wages for others. Those who have gone to the South are rebuilding their former homes with increased hope for the future. They remember their reception at the North, and the efforts made to render them comfortable, and we are already finding them valuable auxiliaries in carrying out our work among the destitute and suffering people of the South.

NECESSITY FOR THE COMMISSION.

LETTERS FROM COMMISSIONERS OF THE BUREAU AND PROVISIONAL GOVERNORS.

Whoever has read with care the preceding pages, must be convinced of the importance of the work in which we are engaged. To illustrate however, the calls which are made upon us, and the manner in which we are welcomed by the loyal men of the South, we append some extracts from a numerous correspondence received at our office.

Maj. Gen. O. O. Howard.—We have given on the inside page of the cover a letter from Gen. HOWARD, endorsing fully the Union Commission. We add an extract from his address, delivered before the Freedmen's Aid Commission, in Chicago, in August last:

"There is another Commission, called the "American Union Commission," I understand the principal object set forth in that, is giving aid to the whites. Well, now, under this Bureau are "refugees," which come first in order, and they are the white people who have been disturbed by the operations of the war. It means all loyal refugees. Now this is taken in its largest sense, and as far as the Government can give aid to these poor, loyal, and ignorant whites, it does it. Now any officers or men who are here, that have been with me through South Carolina, Georgia, Alabama, Tennessee, North Carolina. and Virginia, know very well that there are thousands upon thousands of white people who are suffering. I never have seen people more debased than I found them there. I found many of them with countenances perfectly hopeless, without an apparent object in life—listless. I found multitudes that could not read nor write, no efforts being put forth for their education, none ever thought of. Whatever you may do for the objects of this asssociation, you do well."

Col. Whittlesey, Commissioner of the Freedmen's Bureau for North Carolina, writes us on the 4th of August:

"There is great need of effort in behalf of poor whites in this State, a large number of whom are living in idleness, ignorance, and poverty. I do not know what your plans are for reaching them. *They do not come within the province of this Bureau, since they are not "loyal refugees" nor "Freedmen."* I have, therefore, no work to carry on among them, but if, in any way, I can assist you, I shall be happy to do so."

Gen. R. Saxton Commissioner of the Freedmen's Bureau for South Carolina, writes us:

"Your letter of July 24th, was received here during my temporary absence North. In reply, I can say the field is ample and the laborers few. For a Commission national in its organization, undenominational in its character, including members of all the Christian churches, and catholic in its designs, recognizing no distinction of caste or color in its benefactions, there was never a better opportunity offered for carrying out the objects for which it was constituted. In the three States of South Carolina, Georgia, and Florida, now under my charge, there should be a teacher located on every principal plantation, and hundreds are needed in the towns and cities.

* * * * * * *

"In the interior are needed seeds, agricultural implements of all kinds, food, medicines, and clothing of every description for women and children. Many are now naked, and if they are not provided for before the inclement season, there will be much suffering. Supplies for almost every want incident to humanity are needed,—*scarcely anything will come amiss.*

"The war has left desolation, and with it let us hope freedom in its track. I can find a place for every earnest teacher you can send.

"To rear up in these Southern regions a free Christian State, will require all the missionary energies of the North for a long time to come; and, if we are faithful to the work *now*, in the future these freedmen may in their turn send missionaries to enlighten their brethren in Africa. In behalf of the people and the work now under my charge, I respectfully ask all the aid your Association can render to it and them."

Thomas W. Conway, Commissioner for Louisiana, writes us in August last:

"There are two hundred and fifty thousand Freedmen now in Louisiana, if the most reasonable calculation that can be made at this time by well informed men can be taken as correct, or nearly so. Out of this vast population, nearly one hundred thousand will need clothing the coming winter. This number will be found chiefly in North-Western and North Louisiana, where the benefits of liberty have not yet extended, and where the free labor system has not fully extended.

"There are now fifteen thousand black children educated in this State, under the auspices of this Bureau. There are about three hundred school teachers, and one hundred and fifty schools. The work done in this country now is the greatest that has ever been given to any people heretofore. All the missionary spirit of the American church can, here in the South, find field for its exercise. We need a tide of emigration from the North, such as the North is constantly receiving from Europe. We need honest men, men who while they may desire to make money, should not desire to do so at the expense of the moral and physical welfare of the poor.

"Do all you can to send good teachers."

Gen. C. B. Fiske, Commissioner for the State of Tennessee, writes on the 5th of August:

"I am grateful to you, Sir, for your generous tender to myself of hearty co-operation and aid in the work to which I have been assigned. There is much to do, I assure you, and *it needs to be done now.*

* * * * * * *

"Every citizen of the country should labor to promote the interest of all sections of our united land. I know of no better way to do this than by advancing industrial enterprises, and elevating all classes and colors by the dissemination of virtuous intelligence.

"It will afford me pleasure, while I remain in my present position, to aid you in the judicious distribution of your patriotic gifts to the worthy and necessitous, and you are at liberty to command my service at any time."

Our Reception in the South.—It is not only from the officers of the Bureau we receive such endorsements. The people of the South give us a cordial welcome, and extend to us every facility in their power. They freely offer us the use of their school buildings, as in Knoxville, Raleigh, Macon, and Atlanta. In Richmond, several of the clergy gave us for a time the use of their lecture rooms. Free transportation over the Southern railroads is given to our agents and supplies. Our teachers are not only warmly welcomed but partially supported by the Southern people, who are exerting every energy to give their children educational advantages. The leading Southern newspapers are sent to our central office free of charge. And while we occasionally meet with opposition from some who have not yet recovered from the bitter feelings engendered by the war, we have thus far found ourselves and our proposed work warmly and cordially welcomed by the masses of the Southern people. Some evidence of this feeling we give in the following extracts, from correspondence received by us:

North Carolina—Gov. Holden.

"State of North Carolina Executive Department,
"Raleigh, N. C., *August 7th*, 1865.

"*Rev. Lyman Abbott, New York*,

"Sir:—Your letter of the 25th ult, addressed to His Excellency, Gov. Holden, has been received. His Excellency entirely approves the object of your Association as set forth in your circular and letter, and will take great pleasure in doing anything to promote their success. I have no doubt the proffer made by your Commission will be kindly and gratefully received by North Carolina, the great mass of whose citizens are anxious to bury all past feelings and animosities, and to resume fraternal relations with the Northern people;—indeed there has been in this State throughout the war a strong Union party.

* * * * * * *

"I am, Sir, very respectfully, your obedient servant,
(Signed), "LEWIS HANES,
"Private Secretary to the Governor."

Florida—Gov. Marvin.

"Office of the Provisional Governor,
"Tallahasse, Fla., *Oct. 4th* 1865.

"*Rev. Lyman Abbott*,

"Dear Sir:—I received your letter and the circular of the American Union Commission some weeks since, and referred it to some of the principal citizens of the town. Our State is at present in need of almost every thing, but the people are as hopeful as could be expected, and accept the abolition of slavery and perpetuity of the Union as fixed facts. A good crop next year will do much for them.

"You can do the people of the State service by sending to my address at this place, say two thousand spelling books, and a thousand arithmetics for young beginners, for the use of poor white and colored children. I will undertake their distribution.

"Very respectfully,
(Signed), "WM. MARVIN."

Arkansas.—Gov. Murphy.

"Executive Office,
"LITTLE ROCK, Ark., *Aug. 7th,* 1865.

"*Rev. Lyman Abbott*:—Yours of the 29th July, is received. The American Union Commission is another evidence that the true spirit of Christianity is spreading. Love to our race and kindness to God's creatures,—this is true patriotism;—it is the principle that will render republican government permanent.

"Industry, education, and Christian morality are the pillars of freedom. Our State is a picture of desolation. The great majority of the people are reduced to poverty. The benevolent institutions of the loyal states are producing a right spirit here and softening our hearts, hardened by the terrible scenes and sufferings of the war. The farmers are very destitute of stock and tools, as well as seeds. However, a great exertion has been made to raise something to eat and make something to wear. The people need aid in every way. They need an infusion of Northern example of energy and industry. Emigrants of the proper character would do themselves and us much good. Teachers are much needed, but the people generally are not able to support them. The lands of the State are rich; mineral resources unbounded. The climate as healthy as any other State. All the elements of wealth are here waiting development.

"Kindness will conquer the most stubborn, and reform them if reform is possible. To love our neighbor as ourselves is christianity, is happiness, and is the foundation of all true freedom. The immense efforts of the benevolent institutions of the loyal states have done more to conquer the rebellion than our armies.

"With high respect, &c.,
(Signed), "ISAAC MURPHY."

What answer shall we make to these and similar appeals? How shall we in the name of the North respond to these advances from our fellow-citizens who are striving to secure the restoration of the Union, by re-establishing not merely the government, but those civil and social institutions, and those fraternal feelings which are essential to its perpetuity?

The Freedmen.—We are often asked the question, whether the Union Commission includes the care of the Freedman. We reply emphatically,—

The American Union Commission recognizes no distinction of caste or color. —It is organized to aid the people of the South—not the black men because they are black, nor the white men because they are white, but all men because they are *men*, upon the ground of a common humanity alone. At the same time it has been our constant aim to avoid rivalry of organization and duplication of charities. The President of the Commission is a member of both the American Missionary Society and the National Freedmen's Aid Commission. And it will always be our aim to maintain the most cordial relations and the most hearty co-operation between ourselves and all other organizations laboring in the same field.

The Loyalists of the South.—There are more of them than the people of the North imagine. A wise Christian magnanimity will indeed in the main forget the past, and press forward into the future. It will ask, not chiefly, "What has been?" but, "What is, and shall be?" Nevertheless, those who through all the horrors of a four years war, in spite of violence, misrepresentation and popular prejudice and passion, remained true to the flag and the principles it represented, are peculiarly entitled to a nation's grateful remembrance. There were many such. And of all the people of the South they have been and *still are* the greatest sufferers. In Northern Georgia the most desolate section of the South to day, a secret loyal league was maintained throughout the war. In East Tennessee, it is estimated, fifteen hundred were murdered in cold blood. In Clarksville, the Government gathered 3,000 women and children, last Spring, the families of Union volunteers, recruited in Tennessee, and Northern Georgia and Alabama. The author of "The Secret Service, the Field, the Dungeon and the Escape," Mr. Richardson of the *Tribune*, bears strong testimony to the loyalty of hundreds of the inhabitants in the mountain districts of North Carolina. Are these sufferers to receive no aid and sympathy at our hands? Shall we refuse food to those, who, at peril of their lives, gave it to the Union prisoners? Surely, they ought not to go without some substantial recognition of their patriotic self-devotion. And the Union Commission is the only organization whose constitution allows it to provide succor and relief for them.

AN APPEAL.

We have now set before you our work; we have given you the evidence of its importance and its practicability. Shall we continue it? Shall we, fellow citizens, in your name, and upon your behalf, proffer your sympathy and co-operation to those in the South. who desire to secure the restoration of the Union upon the basis of universal liberty, education, industry, and Christian morality.

We have already aided over 75,000 refugees, to procure homes and employment. We have sent assistance to an incalculable number in their Southern homes. But as winter approaches the distress increases. Will you do anything to relieve it? Will you suffer thousands of your fellow countrymen to perish within the reach of plenty?

We have already aided the people in establishing free schools in the great centres of Nashville, Knoxville, Richmond, and Raleigh. Applications for continued and more extended assistance increases, from parents whose children, unless assisted, must grow up in inevitable ignorance. What answer have the Christian, thoughtful, and patriotic people of the North to make to this request from the Southern masses for our aid and co-operation, in securing for themselves and their children, those educational advantages which should be the birth-right of every American citizen?

The work of war is over. But peace hath its victories no less than war; its conflicts and its duties too. God grant that America may prove equal to that task of restoration and re-building which His Providence has laid upon her.

CONSTITUTION.

ARTICLE I.—The AMERICAN UNION COMMISSION is constituted for the purpose of aiding and coöperating with the people of the United States, which have been desolated and impoverished by the war, in the restoration of their civil and social condition, upon the basis of industry, education, freedom, and Christian morality.

ARTICLE II.—The Commission consists of not less than ten nor more than twenty members, residing in the City of New York and vicinity, together with two representatives from each Branch Commission in other places.

ARTICLE III.—The Commission shall annually elect an Executive Committee of not more than twelve members, who shall have the supervision of its whole work, subject to the direction and approval of the Commission.

ARTICLE IV.—Five members of the Commission constitute a quorum.

ARTICLE V.—The Officers of the Commission are, a President, three Vice-Presidents, a Treasurer, a General Secretary, a Recording Secretary, and such associate Secretaries as shall be elected.

ARTICLE VI.—The Commission, at any regular meeting, may, by a two-third vote, amend the Constitution, except the 1st Article, which may only be altered at the annual meeting, and on previous notice.

BY-LAWS.

I.—THE NATIONAL COMMISSION.

The NATIONAL COMMISSION shall determine the general principles of united action; shall commission all field agents and teachers, direct their operations, and receive monthly reports from them.

The Commission shall meet on the third Monday of every month, for the transaction of regular business; and on the Tuesday preceding the second Thursday of May, for the election of Officers and an Executive Committee. Special meetings may be called by the President or Executive Committee. Every meeting shall be opened with devotional exercises.

II.—BRANCH COMMISSIONS.

Those interested in this work are invited to organize Branch Commissions, or auxiliaries, to be connected with the appropriate Branch. Every Branch will take such means as it deems best in raising funds, procuring supplies, etc., in its own district, but will not initiate movements in the Southern States, except by arrangement with and under the general direction of the Commission. Each Branch shall make a monthly report of its operations to the General Secretary.

III.—THE EXECUTIVE COMMITTEE.

The Executive Committee shall receive the instructions of the Commission at its successive sessions, and be charged with their execution. It will possess all the power of the Commission in the interval of its session, except the power of amending the Constitution and filling vacancies, but its action shall be regularly reported to the Commission, and shall be subject to its revision and correction. It shall hold a weekly meeting for the transaction of business. Special meetings may be called by the Chairman or General Secretary. The unexplained absence of any resident member from three successive sessions of either the Commission or Executive Committee is tantamount to a resignation.

IV.—STANDING COMMITTEES.

The following are the standing Committees of the Commission:—On Finance, Supplies, Agencies, Publication, and Education.

These Committees are elected and vacancies in them filled by the Commission. They are under the general direction of the Executive Committee. Two constitute a quorum.

American Union Commission.

NEW YORK CITY—14 Bible House.

REV. JOSEPH P. THOMPSON, D.D., *Pres.*
REV. LYMAN ABBOTT, *Gen. Sec.*
G. W. LANE, Esq., *Chair. Ex. Com.*
REV. GEO. J. MINGINS, D.D., *Finan. Sec.*
A. V. STOUT, Esq., *Treas.*
H. M. PIERCE, LL.D. *Rec. Sec.*
T. G. ODIORNE, Esq., *Western Secretary*, Cincinnati, Ohio.
WM. A. BOOTH, Esq.
C. C. COLGATE, Esq.
E. L. FANCHER, Esq.
NATHAN BISHOP, L.L.D.
REV. S. H. TYNG, Jr.
REV. WM. IVES BUDDINGTON, D.D.
DAVID DOWS, Esq.
WM. G. LAMBERT, Esq.
HENRY T. MORGAN, Esq.
REV. H. G. WESTON, D.D.
CHAS. BUTLER, Esq.
REV. J. T. DURYEA.
A. A LOW, Esq.
CHRISTOPHER R. ROBERT, Esq.

PHILADELPHIA—1210 Chestnut Street.

SAMUEL V. MERRICK, Esq., *President.*
JOSEPH PARKER, Esq. *Cor. Sec*
SAML. W. WRAY, Esq., *Rec. Sec.*
SAMUEL WORK, Esq., *Treasurer.*
GEORGE G. MEADE, Maj.-Gen. U.S.A.
HON. JAMES POLLOCK.
HON. MORTON Mc MICHAEL.
BENEDICT D. STEWART, Esq.
JOHN WELSH, Esq.
JOSEPH HARRISON, Jr., Esq.
L. MONTGOMERY BOND, Esq.
J. GILLINGHAM FELL, Esq,
ARTHUR G. COFFIN, Esq.
JOHN W. CLAGHORN, Esq.

BOSTON—165 Pearl Street.

HON. MARTIN BRIMMER, *Chair. Ex. Com.*
REV. H. A. MILES, D.D., *Cor. Sec.*
HAMILTON A. HILL, Esq., *Rec. Sec.*
HENRY P. KIDDER, Esq. *Treas.*
DWIGHT FOSTER. Esq.
REV. JOSEPH W. PARKER, D.D.
THOMAS C. WALES, Esq.

BALTIMORE—89 & 91 West Baltimore Street.

G. S GRIFFITHS, Esq., *Pres.*
JOHN N. BROWN, Esq., *Treas.*
REV. F. ISRAEL, *Cor. Sec.*
J. M. FRAZIER, Esq.
REV. C. DICKSON, D.D.
J. C. BRIDGES, Esq,

CHICAGO—90 Washington Street.

C. G. HAMMOND, *Pres.*
REV. J. M. STRONG, *Sec.*
Col. JAMES H. BOWEN, *Treasurer.*
JAMES L. REYNOLDS, Esq.
E. G. HALL, Esq.
REV. H. D. KITCHELL, D.D.
REV. T. M. EDDY, D.D.
REV. W. H. RYDER, D.D.
REV. W. W. PATTEN, D.D.

NEW HAVEN, Connecticut.

Hon. HENRY N. DUBOIS, *Pres.*
REV. D. W. LATHROP, D.D., *Sec.*
PROF L. A. THATCHER, " D. C. GILMAN, M. C. WHITE, M.D., } *Education Committee.*

NASHVILLE, Tennessee.

HON. E ROOT, *Pres.*
REV. R. H. ALLEN, *Cor Sec.*
HON. J. S. FOWLER, *Vice-Pres.*
H. G. SCOVILL, Esq., *Rec. Sec.*
JAMES CAMERON, Esq., *Treas.*

RICHMOND, Virginia.

HORACE L. KENT, Esq., *Pres.*
DAVID TURNER, Esq., *Sec.*
JAMES H. GARDNER, Esq., *Treas.*

www.ingramcontent.com/pod-product-compliance
Lightning Source LLC
LaVergne TN
LVHW011139110826
845150LV00008B/2412
* 9 7 8 1 4 1 8 1 9 3 0 9 6 *